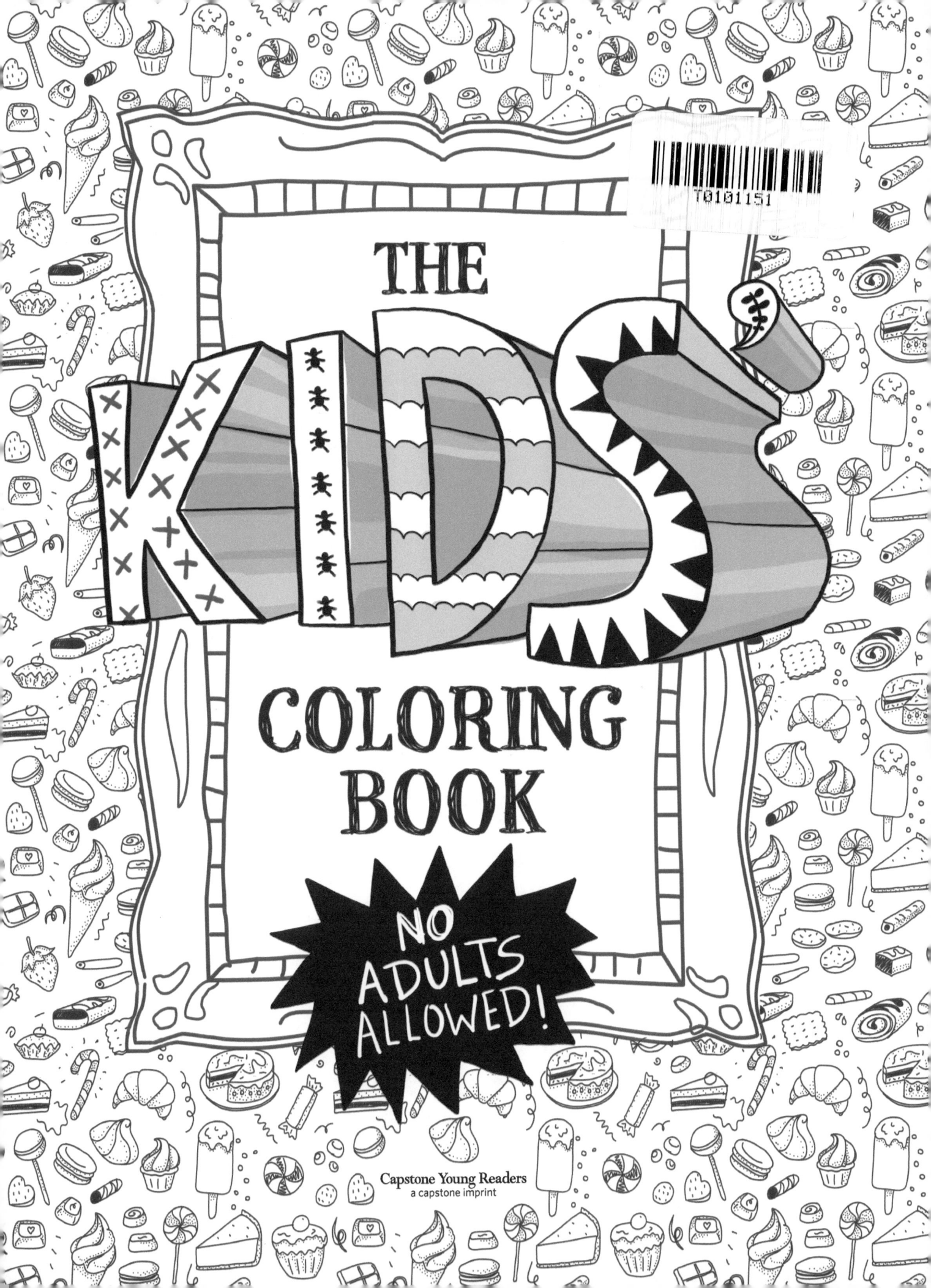
T0101151
THE
KIDS
COLORING
BOOK
NO
ADULTS
ALLOWED!
Capstone Young Readers
a capstone imprint

Published in 2017 by Capstone Young Readers,
A Capstone Imprint
1710 Roe Crest Drive, North Mankato, Minnesota 56003

www.mycapstone.com

Copyright © 2017 by Capstone

All rights reserved. No part of this publication may be reproduced in whole or in part, or stored in a retrieval system, or transmitted in any form or by any means, electronic, mechanical, photocopying, recording, or otherwise, without written permission of the publisher.

Cataloging-in-Publication Data is available on the Library of Congress website.

ISBN: 978-1-62370-856-6 (paperback)

Designers: Aruna Rangarajan and Kay Fraser
Art Director: Heather Kindseth Wutschke
Media Researcher: Jo Miller
Production Specialist: Tori Abraham

Image Credits: Capstone: Bill McGuire, Bob Lentz, Cedric Hohnstadt, Daryll Collins, Dennis Messner, Doug Holgate, Jess Bradley, Lucy Makuc, Steve Harpster; Shutterstock: 100ker, 9george, Alex Rockheart, alfaori, alicedaniel, Anna Bogatirewa, Anna.zabella, Arisa_J, artenot, Artishok, Art'nLera, artplay, AuraLux, Axro, balabolka, Bimbim, blackberry-jelly, blue67design, Brian Goff, Brosko, Buchan, Cat Design, Cerama_ama, Chief Crow Daria, cornflower, Domenick, Drekhann, fraulein_freya, FuzzylLogicKate, Gluiki, handiniatmodiwiryo, Ilya Zonov, ImHope, Incomible, ingaart, Irina Adamovich, IrinaKrivoruchko, IvanNikulin, Julia Henze, Julia Snegireva, Kalenik Hanna, Katerina Pereverzeva, KatiKapik, Kite-Kit, kzhu, Leona Kali, LHF Graphics, lineartestpilot, liskus, Lychy, Magnia, Maryna S, merion_merion, Nadezhda Molkentin, Natalia Chuen, Natalia Sheinkin, natsa, ngocdai86, nicemonkey, Nikolaeva, Nuarevik, Olga_Angelloz, OlichO, Orfeev, pa3x, PAlartist, palform, panki, pzAxe, RetroClipArt, SunshienFlowers, svaga, Teamarwen, tets, totallyjamie, UyUy, Val_Iva, Vanzyst, Vasilixa, Vecster, Vlad Young, Yana Tomashova, YAZZIK, Yevhen Tamavskyi, Yuravector, zelena, zizar, zizi_mentos, zsooofija

Printed in the United States 5669

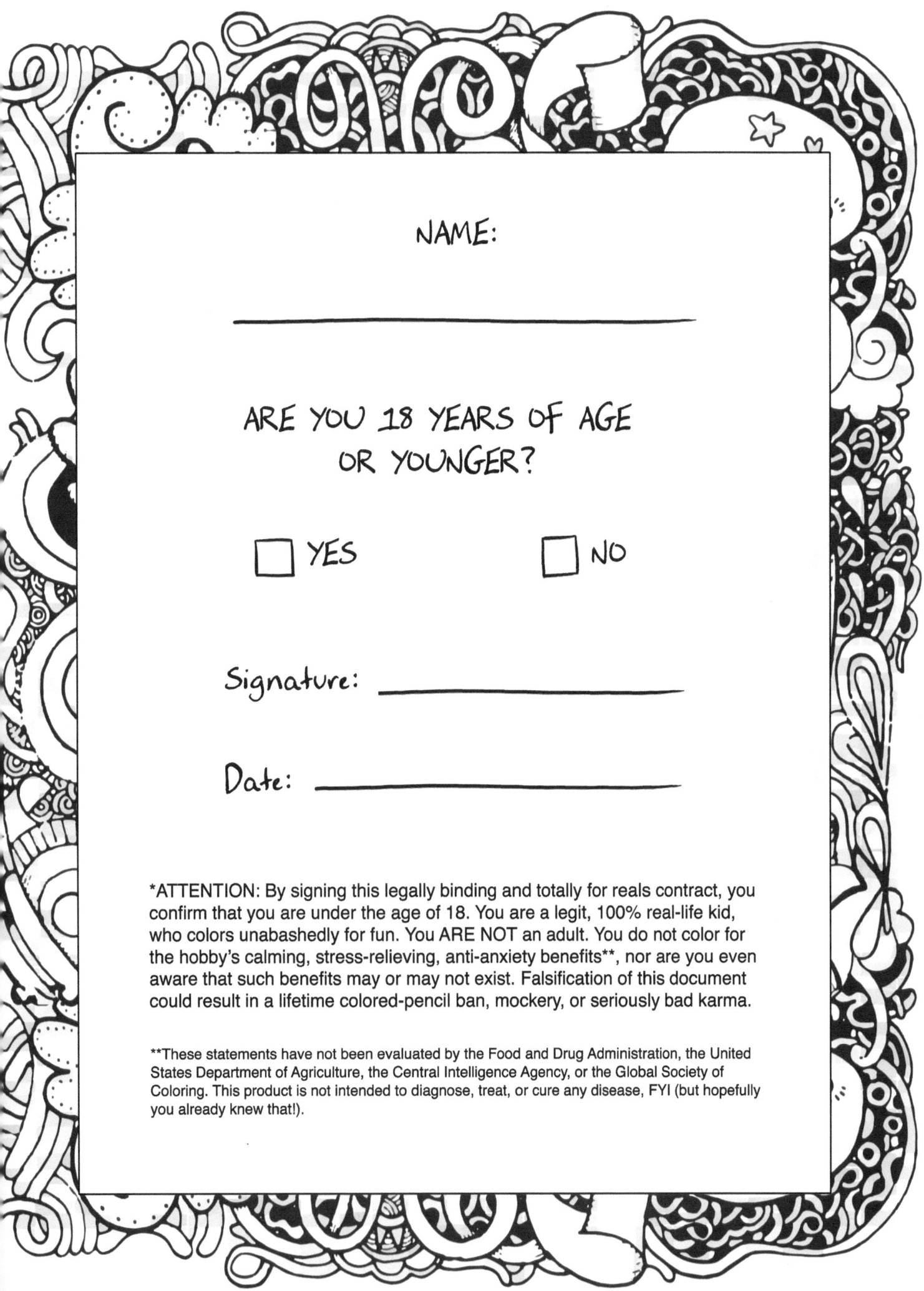

NAME:

_____

ARE YOU 18 YEARS OF AGE OR YOUNGER?

☐ YES ☐ NO

Signature: _____

Date: _____

*ATTENTION: By signing this legally binding and totally for reals contract, you confirm that you are under the age of 18. You are a legit, 100% real-life kid, who colors unabashedly for fun. You ARE NOT an adult. You do not color for the hobby's calming, stress-relieving, anti-anxiety benefits**, nor are you even aware that such benefits may or may not exist. Falsification of this document could result in a lifetime colored-pencil ban, mockery, or seriously bad karma.

**These statements have not been evaluated by the Food and Drug Administration, the United States Department of Agriculture, the Central Intelligence Agency, or the Global Society of Coloring. This product is not intended to diagnose, treat, or cure any disease, FYI (but hopefully you already knew that!).

FYI
OMG
JTLYK
KPC

Dear Adults,

STOP RIGHT THERE!! Put down the colored pencils, turn around, and walk away slowwwwly. This coloring book is NOT. FOR. YOU.

Dear Kids,

Phew! That was close.

As you may have noticed, adults have gone coloring-book crazy these days! They'll color anything within striking distance of their premium, ultra-fine markers: top-secret relaxation gardens, enchanted cat mandalas, calming kaleidoscopes, anti-stress sea animals, and other really, really boring stuff. (Really boring.)

But not this book! No siree! This book is JUST. FOR. YOU.

That's right, boys and girls. Introducing the first-ever adult coloring book for KIDS!

Bust out those old, waxy, broken crayons, and color inside the lines of these awesome illustrations for nothing other than plain-old primary fun! Or — *GASP!* — color OUTSIDE the lines! Who cares?! You're a Kid, after all. Color like one.

Dear Adults,

If you're still reading this (and we know you are)...

KEEP OUT! BACK OFF! STAY AWAY!

This adult coloring book is

FOR KIDS ONLY!

Don't even
THINK
about it, Dad!

MEDITATE
elsewhere,
MOM

MEOW
VASILIXA

ADULTS:
ENTER AT YOUR
OWN RISK!

WHEN YOU'RE IN THE DUMPS...
COLOR!
NO ADULTS ALLOWED

music

DANGER!
KEEP OUT OF
REACH OF ADULTS!!

COLORING
makes me feel
like a kid
(cuz I am one)

KIDS MUST
COLOR

HANDS
OFF MY
COLORING
BOOK!!

POOP
HAV
WEE
UFO
TRASH
COFF
5:30 AM
PIF
PAF
AIR

Just for You
Hello
WOW
123
coffee

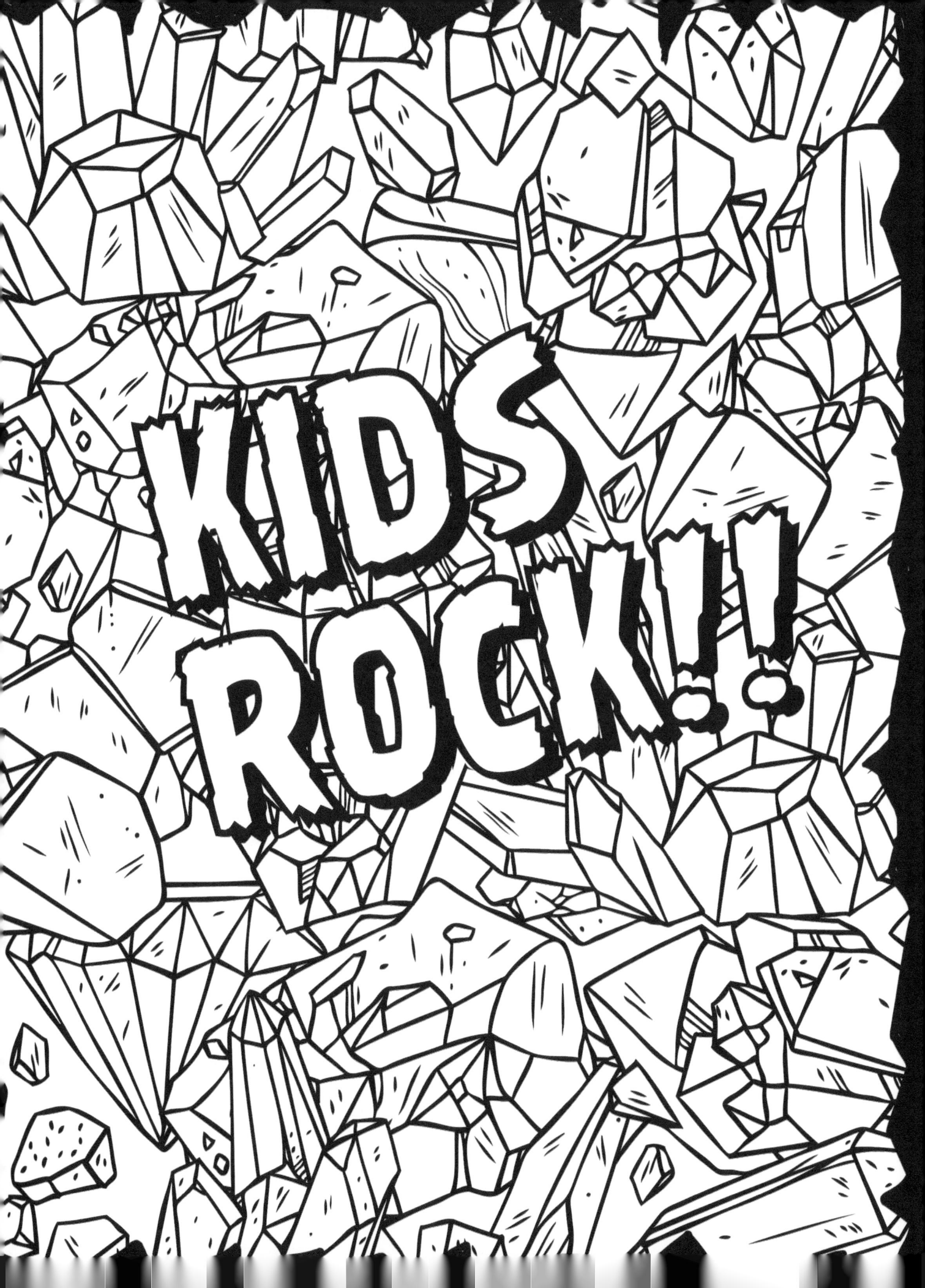
KIDS
ROCK!!

DEAR MOM,
ROSES ARE RED,
VIOLETS ARE BLUE,
THIS COLORING BOOK
ISN'T FOR
YOU.

DINOSAURS don't color. Just sayin'.
T.rex

WHAT'S A MANDALA ANYWAY?

COLOR ME
CALM!
PLEASE!!

I'M NOT MEDITATING.
I'M SPACING OUT!

INTRICATE
CONFUSED
BEWILDERED
DIZZY
FOUL
BUSY

WE
COLOR IN
PEACE!

BE YOUNG
AT ART...
NOT OLD.

WARNING
CONTAINS KID STUFF

Adults may color, but
KIDS
must
COLOR

KEEP YOUR TENTACLES OFF MY COLORING BOOK!

MAKE
coloring
GREAT
AGAIN

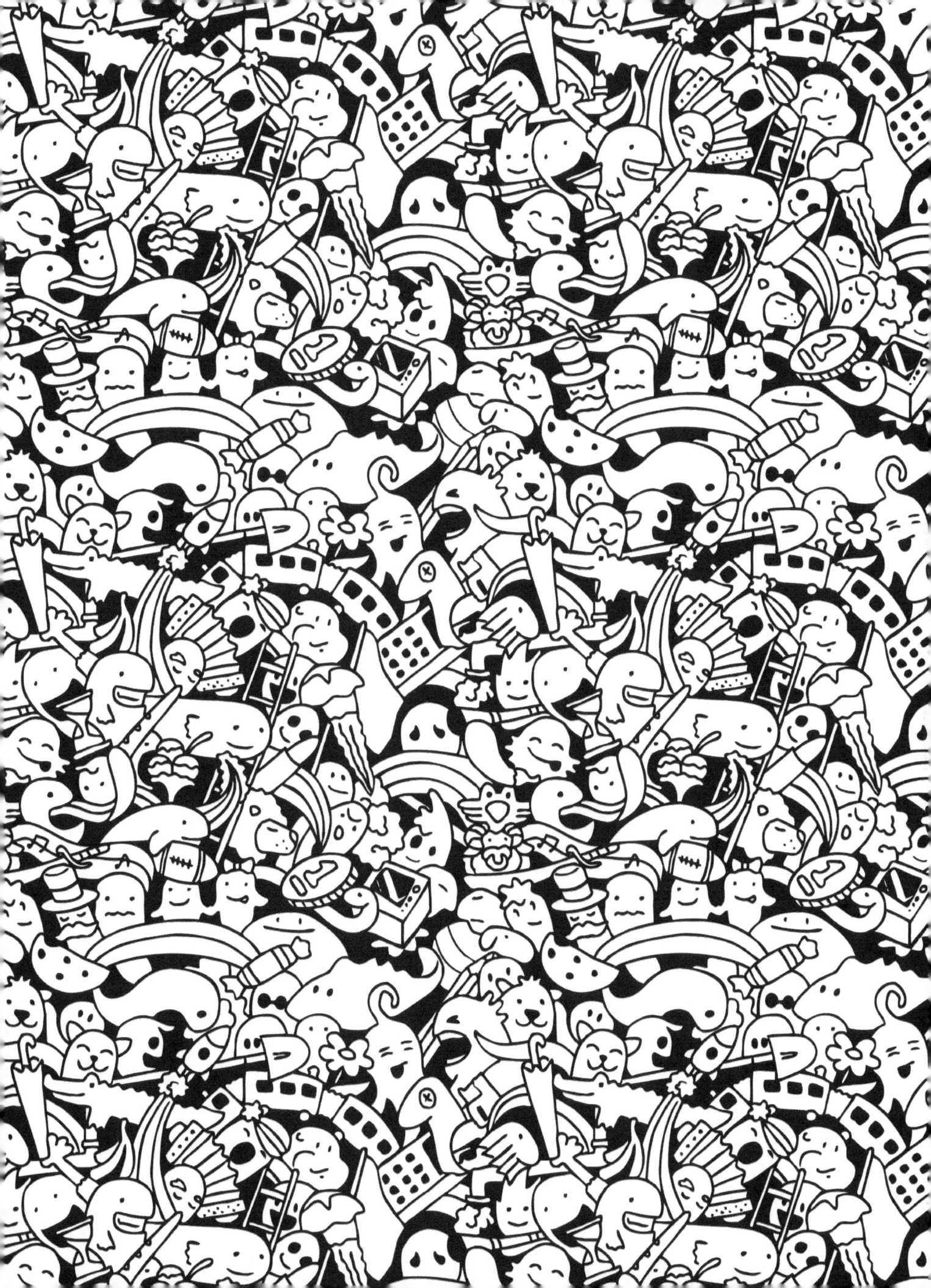

COLOR
LIKE A KID

CRAYONS
ONLY!

PUT AWAY
THE MARKERS,
DAD!

FOR AGES
1 to 100
MINUS AGES
18 to 99

RUFF DAY?
COLOR!

NEVER
SAY
NEVER
(but NEVER color in
this book, Grandpa!)

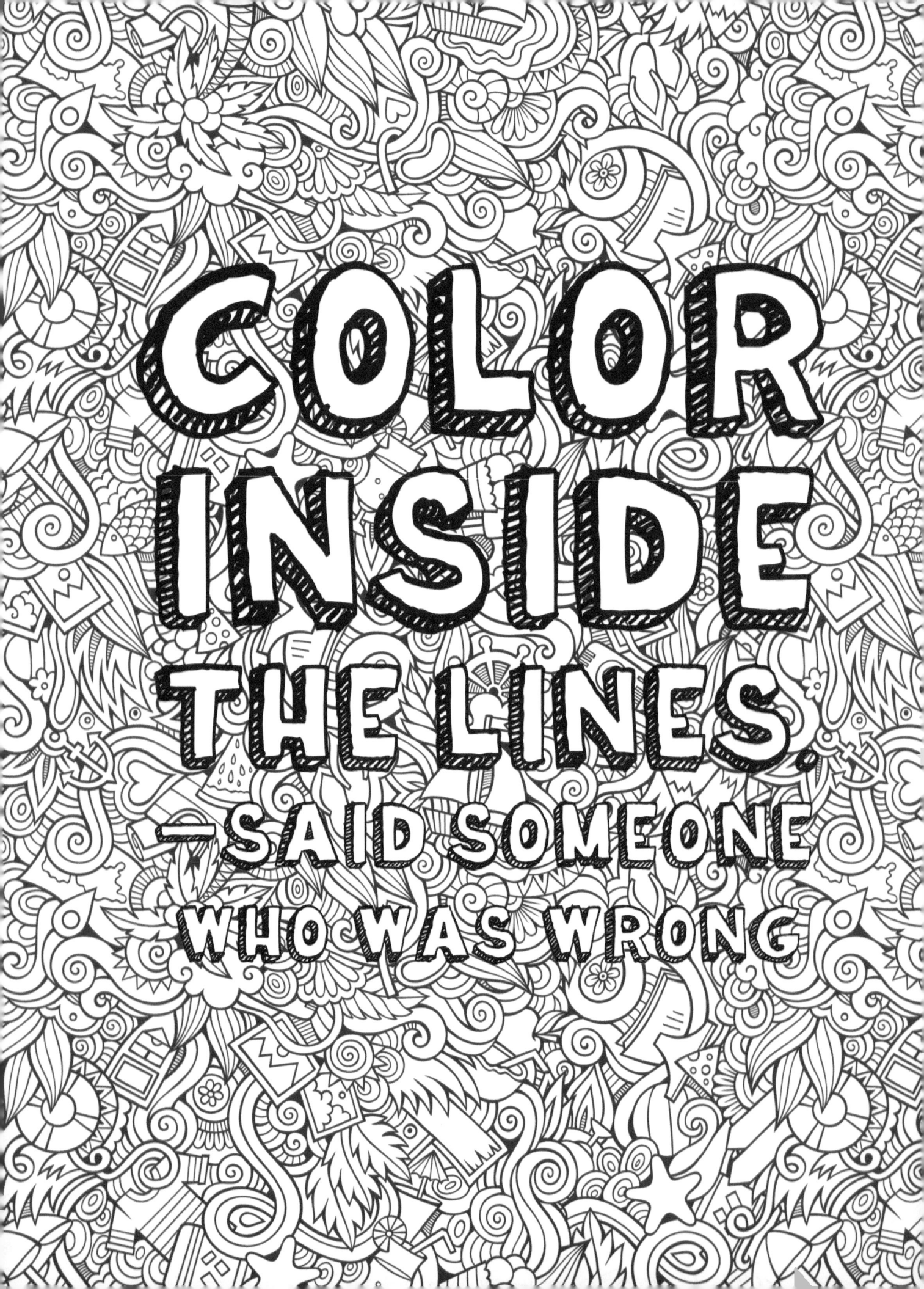
COLOR
INSIDE
THE LINES.
—SAID SOMEONE
WHO WAS WRONG

THIS IS A KIDS-ONLY
SPACE
AREA 52
DESTINATION

I COLOR,
THEREFORE
I AM.

The older
you are,
the better
you color,
said no
one ever.

LISTEN
TO
YOUR
ART
(...when your parents take
away your smartphone)

HI!
#kidstuff
HI!
#... #
#... #

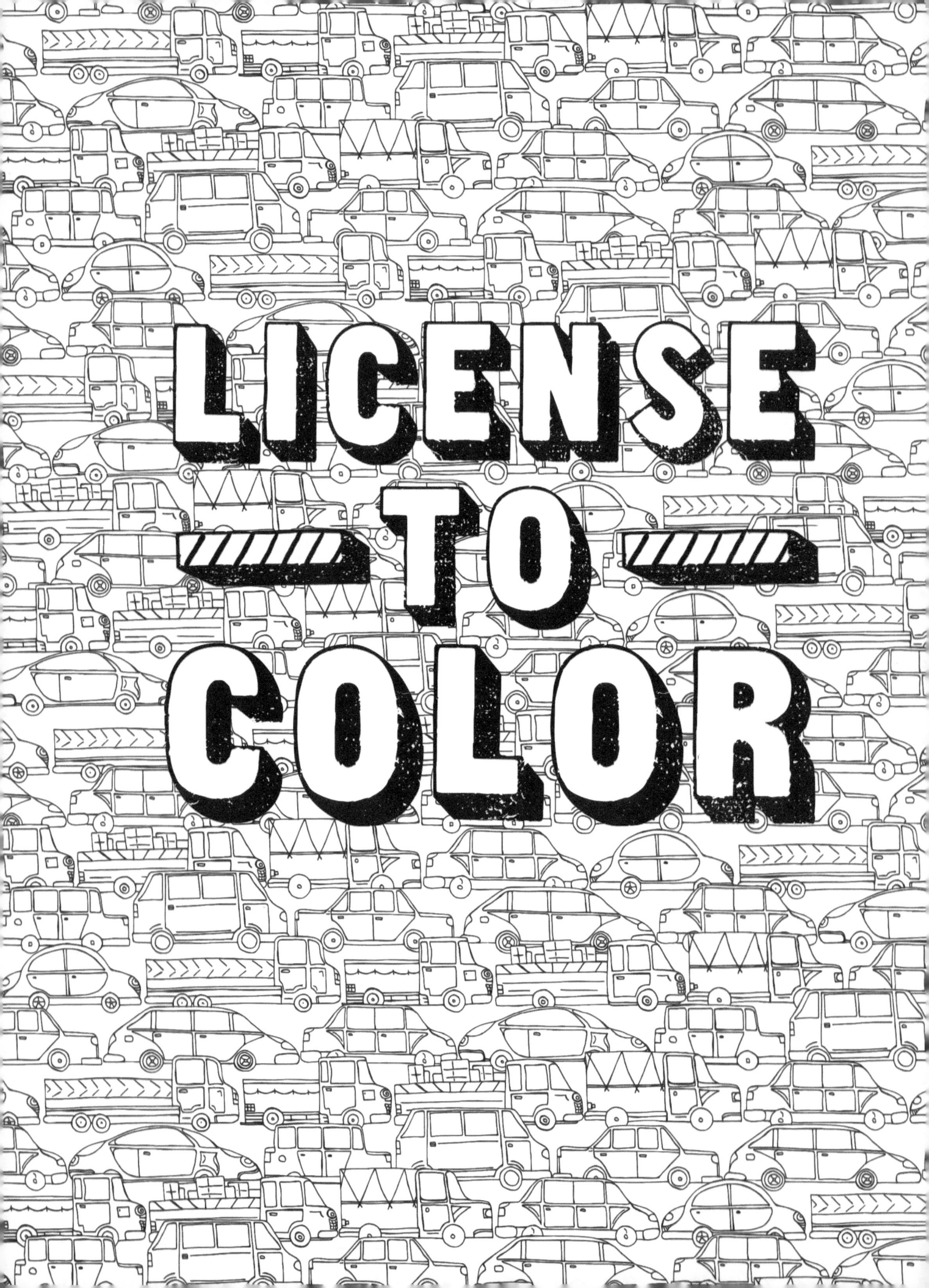
LICENSE
TO
COLOR

RIP
RIP

IF YOU
ARE NOT
A KID...
BUZZ OFF!

COLOR
ME

HELLO MONSTERS!
HELLO MONSTERS!
HELLO MONSTERS!
GRRR
HELLO MONSTERS!
HELLO MONSTERS!
HELLO MONSTERS!
GRRR

P911! PARENT ALERT!

FIND YOUR
OWN
COLORING
BOOK,
GRANDMA

WHAT'S NEXT?
VIDEO
GAMES
FOR ADULTS?

NOT YOUR
FATHER'S
COLORING BOOK

ORANGE YOU GLAD
THAT YOU'RE A KID?

KEEP YOUR PAWS OFF
Mine
Mine Mine Mine
Mine
Mine
Mine
Mine
Mine Mine
Mine
Mine
Mine
Mine
Mine
Mine
Mine
Mine
Mine
Mine
Mine
Mine

SCHOOL
info

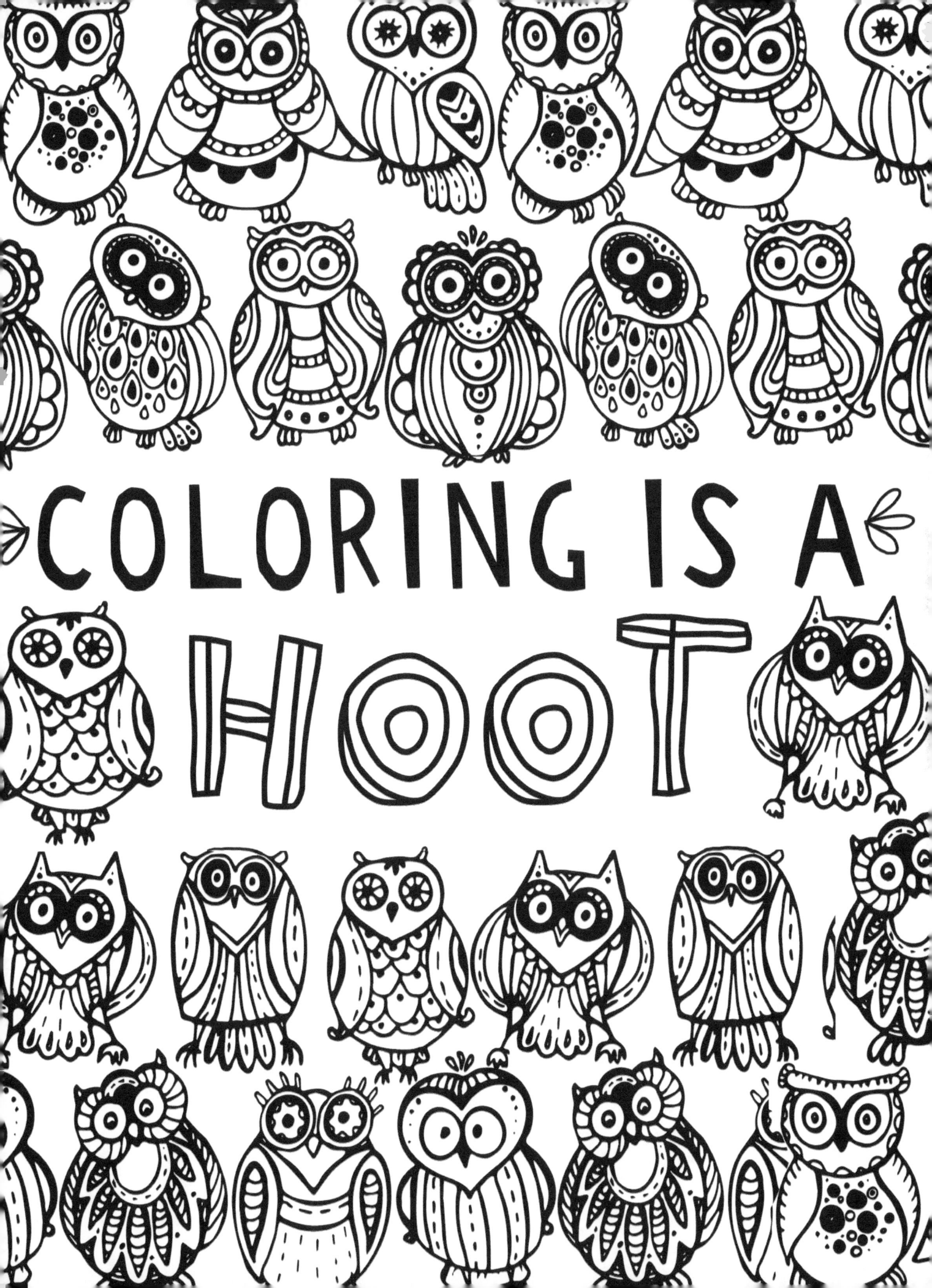
COLORING IS A
HOOT

Don't worry, Dad.
There are other hobbies
IN THE SEA.

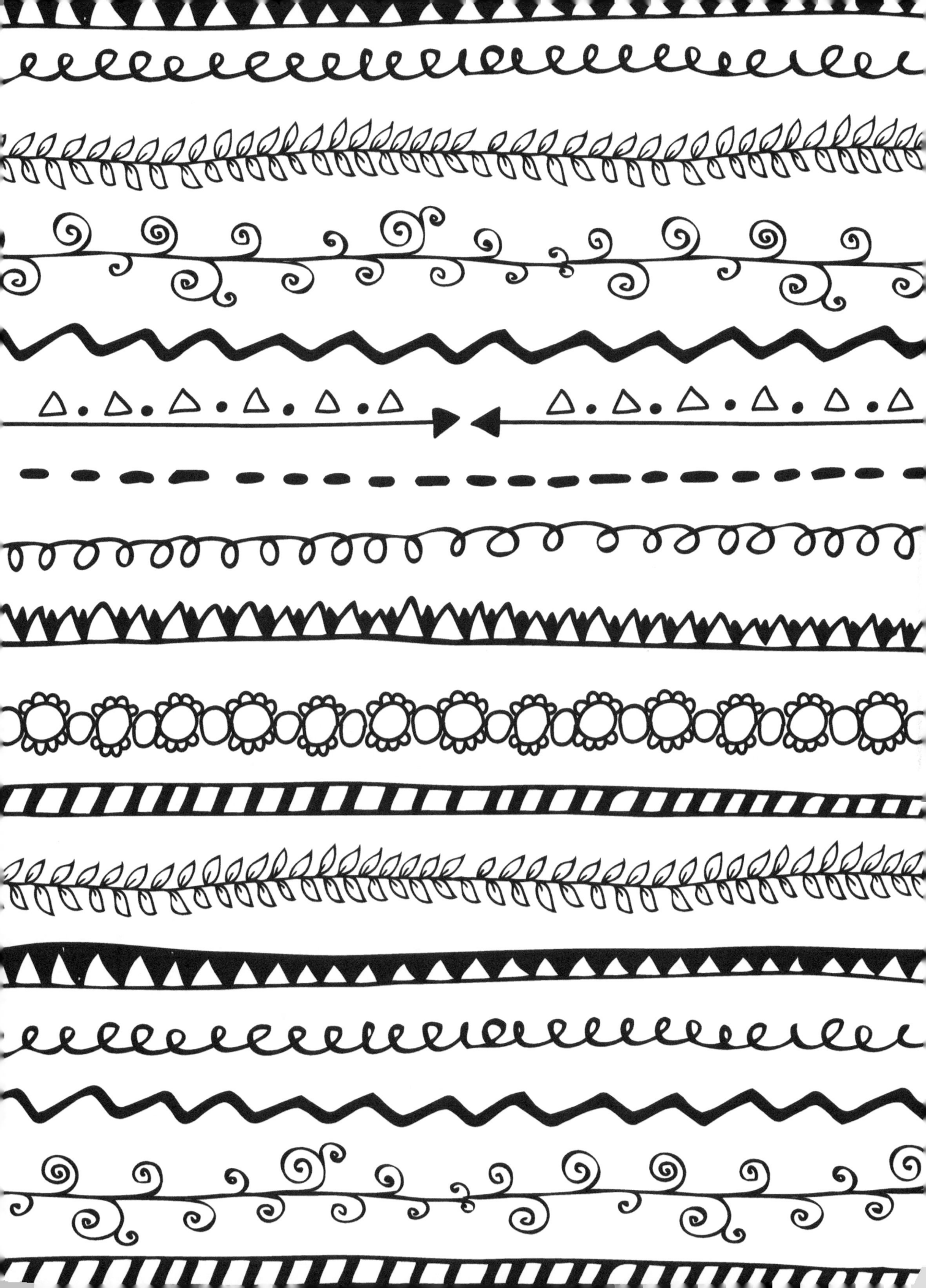

Appetite for Coloring

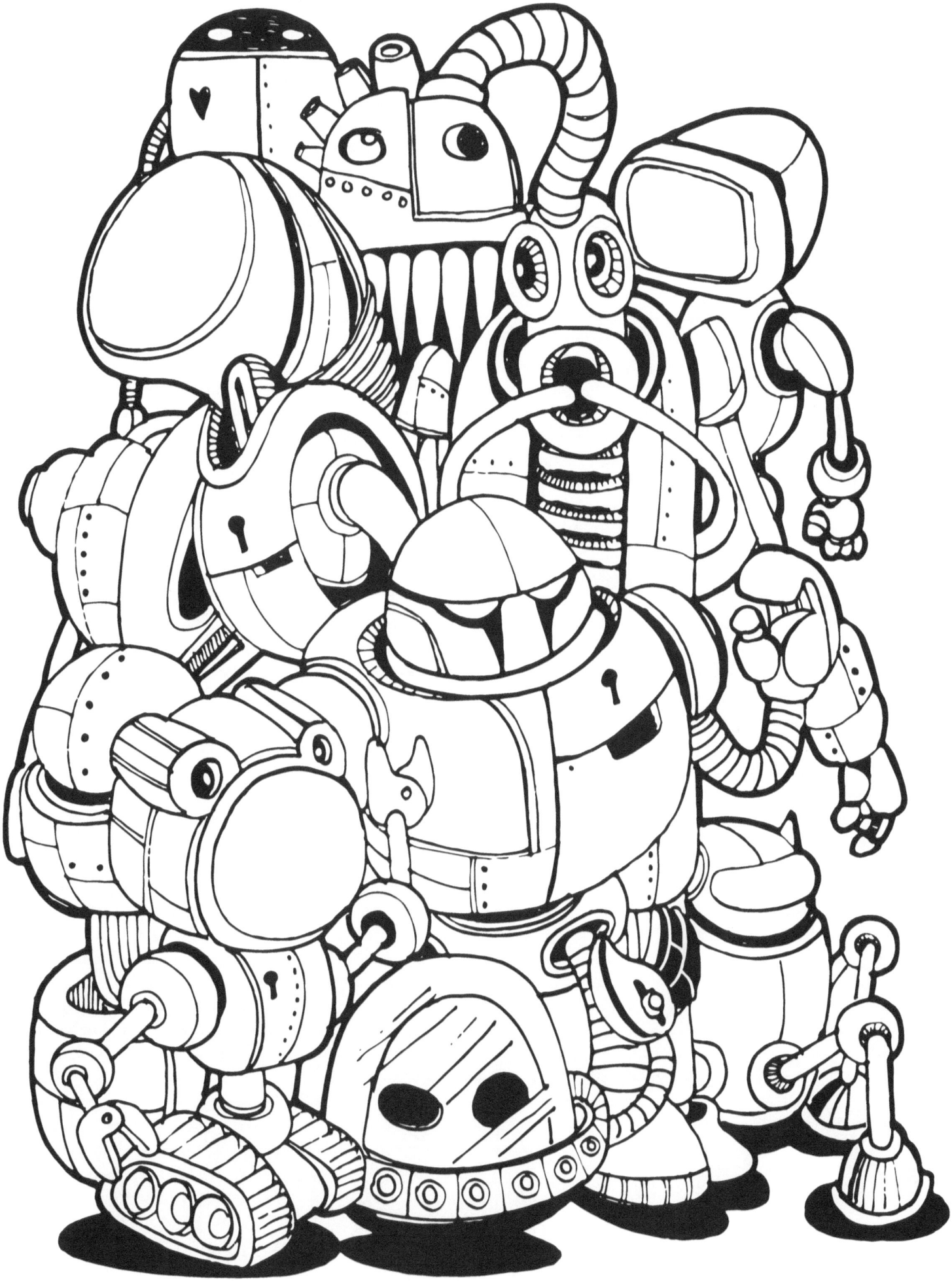

COLORING IS
100% NATURAL...
FOR KIDS

cut along the dotted line

№ 0001

Certificate of achievement

This certificate is awarded to

_____

for successfully proving that

coloring isn't just for adults anymore!*

Date

President, Global Society of Coloring

*If you are an adult, consider this a Certificate of Failure, since you obviously didn't follow directions.

DISCLAIMER

All things appearing in this book are fictional.
Any resemblance to persons living or dead is a
direct result of an over-active imagination.

No adults were harmed in the making of this book.